The Avoid Dance

The Avoid Dance

by Louise Potash

gatekeeper press
Columbus, Ohio

The Avoid Dance
Published by Gatekeeper Press
2167 Stringtown Rd, Suite 109
Columbus, OH 43123-2989
www.GatekeeperPress.com

Library of Congress Control Number: 2021936934

ISBN (hardcover): 9781662910449
ISBN (paperback): 9781662912641
eISBN: 9781662912733

I don't want to fall or spill or miss.

I just feel good
when I'm doing this.

I'll do anything else except something new.

I feel so small

and scared and tight

I duck
and dodge.

And skip and spin.

I hide,

then I seek
the places I've been.

And most of those places
are in my own mind.

They are cozy and comfy
and easy and kind.

The steps I take
to avoid feeling bad

Feel good for a while,

but then leave me sad.

So I'll change my tune
from the Avoid Dance.

I'll feel what I feel.

And wear big kid pants.

CPSIA information can be obtained
at www.ICGtesting.com
Printed in the USA
LVRC090923020921
696552LV00016B/216

9781662910449